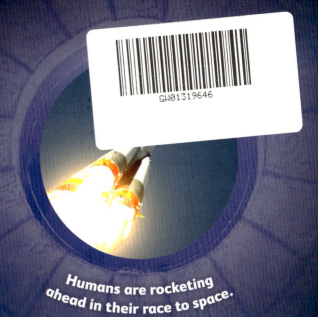

Humans are rocketing ahead in their race to space.

Chapter 1 Alex's Mission Report	2	
Chapter 2 The Space Race Starts	4	
Chapter 3 On the Moon	6	
Chapter 4 Space Life	8	
Chapter 5 Unmanned Exploration	12	
Chapter 6 The Race to Mars	16	
Chapter 7 Search for Life in Space	20	
Chapter 8 Where to Next?	22	

Level 18

"Since my last book, I've returned home to my own planet and written a report about humans in space. It's amazing how much they've achieved!"

Alex the Alien

ALEX'S MISSION REPORT

MISSION REPORT
AUTHOR: ALEX THE ALIEN
TOPIC: EARTHLINGS' SPACE RACE

Greetings, fellow aliens — and thank you for this welcome-home celebration. As you know, many years ago, I travelled to planet Earth. My mission was to observe the advances that humans were making in their race to space.

I can report that in only sixty Earth years, humans have had great success with their space missions. Now, they're planning manned missions to other planets in their solar system, such as Mars. Here is my report on their exciting space exploration activities!

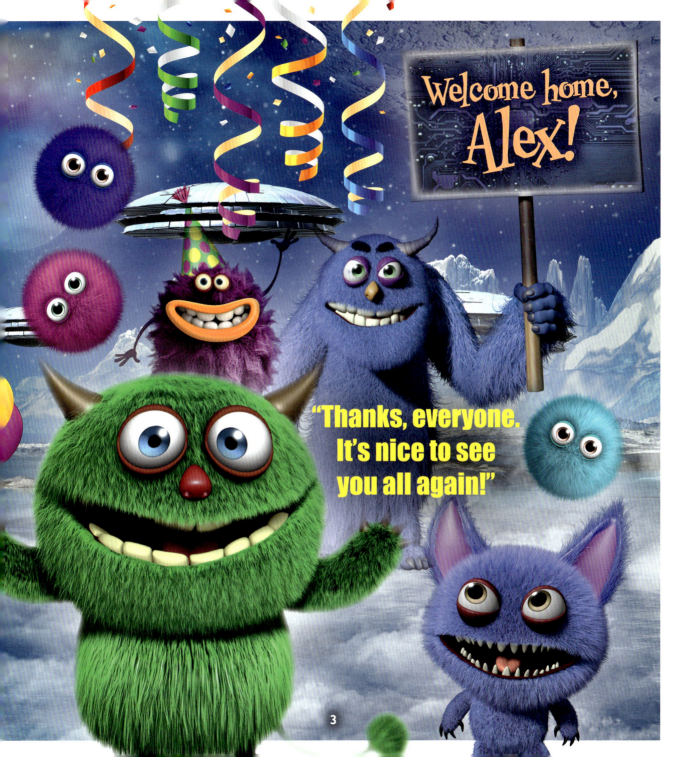

2 THE SPACE RACE STARTS

MISSION REPORT
AUTHOR: ALEX THE ALIEN
TOPIC: EARLY YEARS OF THE SPACE RACE

Robert Goddard was a space rocket pioneer. As a boy in the USA, he dreamed of building something that could fly to Mars. In 1926, Goddard launched the first liquid-fuelled rocket. It flew for two-and-a-half seconds and reached an altitude of 12 metres.

In the years after Goddard's first rocket, better rockets were developed. By 1957, they had improved so much that a Russian rocket carried *Sputnik 1*, the first satellite, into space. And, in 1961, Yuri Gagarin became the first human in space.

Robert Goddard launched his rocket on 16 March, 1926, from his aunt's farm in Massachusetts, USA.

During World War 2 (1939–45), rockets that could reach an altitude of 88 kilometres were built.

Sputnik 1 was the first space satellite. It orbited Earth at 29 000 kilometres per hour for three months in 1957.

The first human in space, Yuri Gagarin, orbited Earth at an altitude of more than 300 kilometres in 1961.

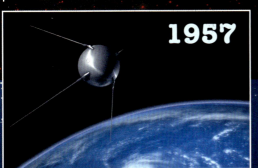

ON THE MOON

MISSION REPORT
AUTHOR: ALEX THE ALIEN
TOPIC: FOOTSTEPS ON THE MOON

On 20 July 1969, an American astronaut named Neil Armstrong said these words:

"That's one small step for man, one giant leap for mankind."

He had just become the first human to step onto the moon. Soon after, another astronaut, Buzz Aldrin, joined Armstrong. The astronauts explored the moon's surface for 20 hours, before returning to Earth with their third crew member, Michael Collins.

Between 1969 and 1972, 11 more astronauts explored the moon's dry, dusty surface.

Neil Armstrong (1930–2012) was the first human to walk on the moon.

Apollo 11

The first mission to the moon was called Apollo 11. On 16 July 1969, a powerful Saturn 5 rocket launched three astronauts into space – Neil Armstrong, Buzz Aldrin and Michael Collins. On top of the rocket were two smaller spacecraft, which flew towards the moon. One of these spacecraft (*Eagle*) landed on the moon, while the other (*Columbia*) orbited above. After their mission, *Columbia* carried the three astronauts back to Earth. They returned safely on 24 July 1969.

The Apollo 11 Saturn 5 lifts off from the USA (left).

Eagle starts its descent to the moon (below).

4 SPACE LIFE

MISSION REPORT
AUTHOR: ALEX THE ALIEN
TOPIC: LIVING IN SPACE

Space travel is a great achievement for humans. But staying alive in space is a great challenge.

Humans need air, water and food to survive. They had to design and build spacecraft and space suits that would keep them alive. Humans are also used to gravity so they had to train in zero-gravity conditions before going into space.

By 2000, space agencies from around the world had built an International Space Station. Since then, astronauts from many countries have visited the space station to learn more about living in space and to do experiments.

Space Suits

When astronauts leave their spacecraft, they must wear space suits. Space suits are like mini-spacecraft, with everything an astronaut needs to survive built into them.

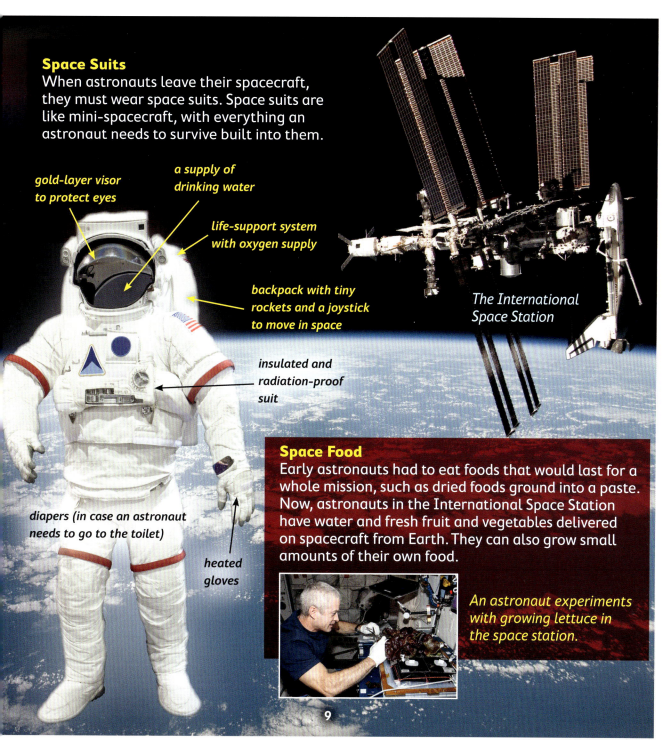

- gold-layer visor to protect eyes
- a supply of drinking water
- life-support system with oxygen supply
- backpack with tiny rockets and a joystick to move in space
- insulated and radiation-proof suit
- diapers (in case an astronaut needs to go to the toilet)
- heated gloves

The International Space Station

Space Food

Early astronauts had to eat foods that would last for a whole mission, such as dried foods ground into a paste. Now, astronauts in the International Space Station have water and fresh fruit and vegetables delivered on spacecraft from Earth. They can also grow small amounts of their own food.

An astronaut experiments with growing lettuce in the space station.

Space Shuttles

For many years, NASA space shuttles were used to take space station parts, supplies and new crew members to the International Space Station. They are no longer used.

Five space shuttles were built. Between 1981 and 2011, they flew 135 space missions.

Today, spacecraft from the USA, Russia, Japan and Europe take supplies and crew to the space station.

A space shuttle launches from Florida, USA.

Countries Work Together
Spacecraft from many countries bring supplies to the space station. This Soyuz spacecraft is from Russia.

Zero-Gravity Training
Training underwater helps astronauts get used to living in zero gravity before going to the space station.

Repairs Outside
To make repairs to the space station, astronauts often have to work outside. They are safely tethered to the station.

Sleep Standing Up
So they don't float around, most astronauts prefer to sleep upright, in sleeping bags attached to the walls.

UNMANNED EXPLORATION

MISSION REPORT
AUTHOR: ALEX THE ALIEN
TOPIC: UNMANNED SPACE EXPLORATION

Technology has enabled humans to explore places that, at the moment, they could never travel to.

Humans have landed unmanned space probes on the planets Venus and Mars. Probes have explored icy comets in their solar system, too.

In 1977, two space probes, *Voyager 1* and *2*, were launched to explore different parts of space. *Voyager 1* is now in deep space beyond the solar system, almost 20 billion kilometres from home. And *Voyager 2* is heading for deep space, too! Let's discover more about *Voyager 1*.

Voyager 1

For almost 40 years, *Voyager 1* travelled past planets in the solar system, sending photographs and other data back to Earth. Then, in 2012, it left the solar system and continued on into deep space.

Scientists expect *Voyager 1* will keep sending information back to Earth until 2025.

(right) Voyager 1 is launched into space in 1977.

(right) Voyager 1 journeys beyond the solar system.

Greetings from Earth

In case *Voyager 1* or *2* are ever discovered by other life forms, they are carrying gold-plated records with greetings in 55 languages. There are recordings of whales, a baby crying, waves breaking on the shore and music from many cultures. The record also contains images and information about Earth. Symbols show how to play the record, too.

Jupiter

Jupiter's surface

Jupiter
The largest planet in the solar system is Jupiter. When *Voyager 1* travelled past it in 1979, humans were amazed by the photos it took of Jupiter's surface and its moons.

VOYAGER 1 – JOURNEY SO FAR

The Sun *Mercury* *Venus* *Earth* *Mars* *Jupiter*

Saturn
Voyager 1 also explored Saturn and its rings in 1980, before travelling past Uranus, Neptune and Pluto and on into deep space.

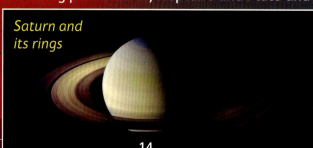
Saturn and its rings

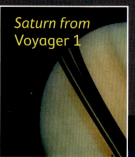
Saturn from Voyager 1

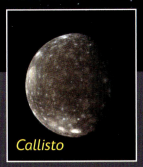
Callisto

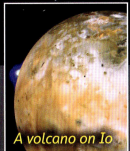
A volcano on Io

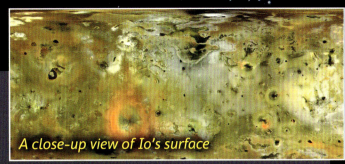
A close-up view of Io's surface

Jupiter's Moons

Jupiter has 67 moons orbiting it. Photos and data from *Voyager 1* allowed humans to see many of the moons, such as Callisto and Io, close-up for the first time. Most are rocky and frozen, but some have active volcanoes and rugged landscapes.

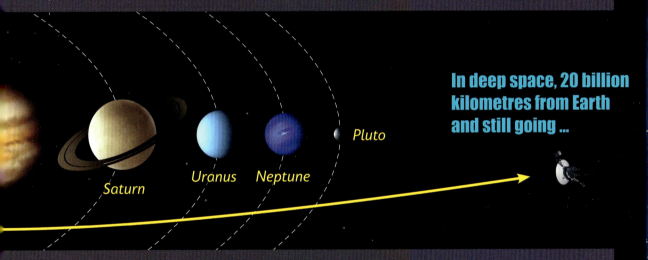

Saturn — *Uranus* — *Neptune* — *Pluto*

In deep space, 20 billion kilometres from Earth and still going ...

Saturn's Rings and Moons

Voyager 1 helped humans discover at least 95 separate rings surrounding Saturn. The rings are mostly made up of ice, dust and rocks. Saturn also has 62 moons.

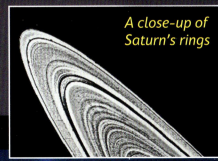
A close-up of Saturn's rings

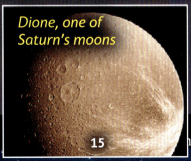
Dione, one of Saturn's moons

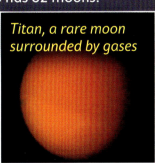
Titan, a rare moon surrounded by gases

6 THE RACE TO MARS

MISSION REPORT
AUTHOR: ALEX THE ALIEN
TOPIC: LIVING ON MARS

In 2015, humans announced that their Mars Reconnaissance Orbiter had discovered signs of water on Mars. This was a very exciting discovery, as water is needed for life to exist.

If water exists on Mars, humans might be able to survive there — but only if they can find enough water to drink and grow plants.

Until now, humans have only sent unmanned "rovers" to do experiments and to explore the surface of Mars. But now, with signs of water, the race is on to send astronauts to Mars and return them safely home.

Mars has a red, brownish surface with sand and rocks.

Mars

This image shows streaks and gullies on Mars – features made by flowing water.

Mars Exploration

Mars has always fascinated humans. For many years, they have wondered if life exists on this planet.

Since the 1960s, many unmanned spacecraft have travelled to Mars. In 1971, the Russians successfully landed a probe on the Martian surface.

In 1976, two American probes, *Viking 1* and *Viking 2*, landed on Mars. They took many photographs, reported on the weather and performed a number of experiments.

In 2006, the Mars Reconnaissance Orbiter reached Mars. This spacecraft still orbits Mars, looking for water.

The Mars Science Laboratory landed on Mars in 2012. The laboratory is in a car-sized rover that explores the surface. The rover, called *Curiosity*, is still working. It conducts experiments to find out if the Martian environment could have ever supported life.

The Mars rover, Curiosity

Planning an Expedition to Mars

Space agencies already have plans to travel to Mars and explore the planet by 2030. But there are several challenges.

Astronauts on a Mars mission would have to spend at least three years in space, which might affect their health. More powerful spacecraft are needed to carry enough food and water for such a long journey. And, once they arrive, astronauts would need protection against the harsh Martian environment.

Nevertheless, scientists are now looking for good landing sites. Engineers are designing spacecraft technology for a Mars mission. Soon, humans will set foot on another planet for the first time.

A NASA artist's design of a plastic spacecraft.

Plastic Spacecraft to Mars?

The millions of plastic bags that end up as rubbish each year may hold the key to keeping astronauts healthy.

Scientists have discovered that this type of plastic can be used to make spacecraft. The plastic is light and strong enough to build spacecraft that can protect astronauts from dangerous space radiation. NASA engineers are exploring the possibility of building a plastic spacecraft for the journey to Mars!

A NASA artist's impression of how humans might look while exploring Mars.

SEARCH FOR LIFE IN SPACE

MISSION REPORT
AUTHOR: ALEX THE ALIEN
TOPIC: EXTRATERRESTRIAL LIFE

Humans have always wondered if there was life anywhere else in the universe. By the 1970s, advances in technology meant they could start looking.

Large radio telescopes, which can detect electronic signals, are listening for signals from space. And, around the world, thousands of home computers are linked together to form a powerful supercomputer that checks the data from the radio telescopes.

But there is one thing humans haven't figured out yet: what they will do if they *do* discover life!

SETI
The Search for Extraterrestrial Intelligence (SETI) uses hundreds of radio telescopes, pointing at different parts of space. SETI scientists listen for noise patterns that might be a sign of alien life. Nothing has been found so far.

Space Telescope
Since 1990, the Hubble Space Telescope has orbited above Earth, taking amazing photos of distant galaxies. It also helps astronomers find distant planets that might have similar environments to those found on Earth.

A radio telescope (right) collects electronic data from parts of space too distant to be seen with ordinary telescopes.

(right) Three Hubble photos of distant stars and galaxies.

8 WHERE TO NEXT?

MISSION REPORT
AUTHOR: ALEX THE ALIEN
TOPIC: CONCLUSION

In conclusion, I can report that humans have made amazing advances in space exploration. And, with better technology and increased knowledge, their space race is speeding up.

Humans have walked on Earth's moon. Astronauts are living in space. Their rovers are exploring Mars. Two *Voyager* spacecraft probes are in deep space beyond Earth's solar system.

And sooner or later, humans may discover that they share their universe with other life forms.

So, we had better be prepared!

... may be our space visitors of tomorrow!

Will You Be the First?
NASA's mission to Mars is scheduled for 2030. That means that somewhere on Earth, right now, there are students who might be the first humans to walk on another planet! Could *you* be one of them?

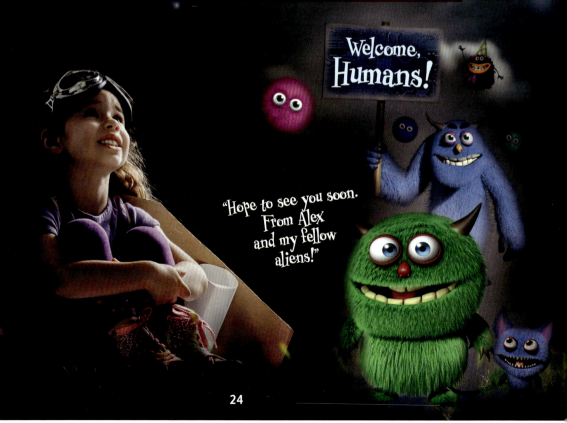

Welcome, Humans!

"Hope to see you soon. From Alex and my fellow aliens!"